GW00732968

WHATEVER HAPPENED TO MARRIAGE?

Patrick Treacy SC

All booklets are published
thanks to the generosity of the supporters
of the Catholic Truth Society

All biblical quotations are taken from the New Revised Standard Version.

ISBN 978 1 78469 575 0

Summary

Speaking in Tbilisi, Georgia, on 1st October 2016, Pope Francis said that "today, there is a global war trying to destroy marriage....[T]hey don't destroy it with weapons, but with ideas." This booklet explores the ideas that are destroying marriage.

In the first part, the true nature of marriage is set out, as understood by the Catholic Church, based upon biblical revelation and the objective nature of the human person.

The second part of the booklet then explores a precise description of the problem defined by Pope Francis in his Apostolic Exhortation On Love in the Family, *Amoris Laetitia* (2016), in which he says: "Many countries are witnessing a legal deconstruction of the family, tending to adopt models based almost exclusively on the autonomy of the individual will."

The third and final part of the booklet then explains the five ideas of excarnation, gender theory, equalism, dehumanised rights and adolescent progressivism that have facilitated a false understanding of marriage to gain currency in Western societies.

Contents

"Today, there is a global war trying to destroy marriage....[T]hey don't destroy it with weapons, but with ideas.

"It's certain ideological ways of thinking that are destroying it."

Pope Francis, Tbilisi, Georgia
1st October 2016

Introduction:
An overview of what
has happened to marriage

In the book of Genesis, the very first attack of the serpent is upon the intimacy of man and woman. Initially, "the man and his wife were both naked, and were not ashamed" (*Gn* 2:24). The serpent attacks their nakedness, the essence of their intimacy and their bodies, which form their marital union. Once the serpent succeeds with this first attack, which is upon marriage, "the eyes of both were opened, and they knew that they were naked; and they sewed fig leaves together and made loin clothes for themselves" (*Gn* 3:7).

The purpose of this booklet is to explain the most recent attack upon marriage between a man and woman. It explores how the true and unchanging meaning of marriage has been manipulated by false ideas which have led to the distortion of the truth of what marriage is. The pontificate of Pope Francis has been unfailing in highlighting how serious this confusion about the true nature of marriage is.

Pope Francis gave clear expression to this concern during his first visit to the United States of America in September 2015. On 23rd September 2015, Pope Francis gave his first address of his visit at the White House. He said: "I will also travel to Philadelphia for the Eighth World Meeting of Families, to celebrate and support the institutions of marriage and the family at this, a critical moment in the history of our civilisation." On the following day, in the course of his address to the Joint Session of the United States Congress, Pope Francis said: "I cannot hide my concern for the family, which is threatened, perhaps as never before, from within and without. Fundamental relationships are being called into question, as is the very basis of marriage and the family." In his speech to the American Bishops at St Charles Borromeo Seminary in Philadelphia on the morning of 27th September 2015, being the final day of his visit to the United States, he said: "Until recently, we lived in a social context where the similarities between the civil institution of marriage and the Christian sacrament were considerable and shared. The two were interrelated and mutually supportive. This is no longer the case."

From the outset, it should be stated that one does not need to regard marriage as a sacrament and a vow before God in order to adhere to the view that it is based on the distinction as to sex between man and woman. In every society of which records exist, marriage is seen as a bond between man and woman, in which the whole of society has an interest, for the bearing of children and the preparation for family life lie at the heart of the marital tie.

This understanding of marriage is also anchored in the very beginning of the Old Testament and explicitly affirmed in the New Testament. In the first book of the Old Testament, the Book of Genesis, we read: "So God created humankind in his image, in the image of God he created them; male and female he created them" (*Gn* 1:27).

In the second chapter of the Book of Genesis, it is written: "Therefore a man leaves his father and his mother and clings to his wife, and they become one flesh" (*Gn* 2:24).

In Chapter 19 of the Gospel of St Matthew, Jesus is recorded as having an encounter with the Pharisees which is described in this way:

> Some Pharisees came to him, and to test him they asked, "Is it lawful for a man to divorce his wife for any cause?" He answered, "Have you not read that the one who made them at the beginning 'made them male and female,' and said, 'For this reason a man shall leave his father and mother and be joined to his wife, and the two shall become one flesh'? So they are no longer two, but one flesh. Therefore what God has joined together, let no one separate." (*Mt* 19:3-6)

Furthermore, this booklet does not consider the effect of divorce upon our understanding of marriage. It is concerned with the seismic change which has taken place to our understanding of marriage since the beginning of this millennium. The existence of divorce does not fundamentally change the nature of marriage in the manner that has only occurred since the beginning of the twenty-first century.

This change is to say that whether the two parties to the marriage are a man and a woman or not is a matter of indifference. The purpose of this booklet is to understand why this has occurred and why it is based upon a false understanding of marriage and of the human person.

In 2000 the Netherlands was the first country to enact legislation providing for civil marriage between two persons of the same sex, and it came into force in 2001. By the end of 2017, civil marriage between two people of the same sex was legally recognised (nationwide or in some parts) in twenty-two countries, namely Argentina, Australia, Belgium, Brazil, Canada, Colombia, Denmark, Finland, France, Germany, Iceland, the Republic of Ireland, Luxembourg, Malta, Mexico, the Netherlands, New Zealand, Norway, Portugal, South Africa, Spain, Sweden, the United Kingdom, the United States and Uruguay.

The Republic of Ireland is the only country to introduce same-sex marriage into its civil law by means of a popular referendum which directly amended its Constitution to provide for it. This led to the insertion of an article into the Irish Constitution (Article 41.4) which provides: "Marriage may be contracted in accordance with law by two persons without distinction as to their sex."

This simple wording encapsulates the essence of the change which has taken place in the understanding of marriage in the laws of these countries. In their civil laws, marriage no longer has anything to do with the distinction as to sex between man and woman. It has been decoupled from the fixed, unchanging biological differences between both. This change in the legal understanding of marriage is, therefore, rooted in an even more fundamental change, which is that the distinction as to sex between a man and a woman does not deserve separate legal recognition in these societies. Even though it is only through a man and a woman that another human being can be procreated and even though the cells of our bodies are comprised from the genetic material from both our mothers and our fathers, marriage is no longer given a separate status based on the distinction as to sex between a man and a woman.

Accordingly, this booklet approaches this problem in three parts. In its first part, the true nature of marriage is set out, as understood by the Catholic Church, based upon biblical revelation and the objective biological nature of the human person. The second part of the booklet then explores a precise description of the problem defined by Pope Francis in his Apostolic Exhortation On Love in the Family, *Amoris Laetitia* (2016), in which he says: "Many countries are witnessing a legal deconstruction of the family, tending to adopt models based almost exclusively on the autonomy of the individual will" (*AL* 53). The third and final part of the booklet then explains the five ideas of excarnation, gender theory, equalism, dehumanised rights and adolescent progressivism that have facilitated a false understanding of marriage to gain currency in Western societies.

Part One:
The true nature of marriage

---

1. The understanding of marriage
of the Catholic Church

The Catholic Church's understanding of marriage is expressed in Canons 1055 and 1056 of the *Code of Canon Law*,[1] as it is in a central document of the Second Vatican Council, *Gaudium et Spes*.[2] Taken together, these authorities express the Church's understanding of marriage as an intimate, exclusive and indissoluble communion of man and woman, designed by God, the Creator, for their good and the procreation and education of children. As a covenant between two baptised persons, it has been raised by Jesus Christ to the dignity of a sacrament.

The Church itself can be understood as a love story between God and humanity that is urged by the Holy Spirit towards unity. The heart of this story is the Gospels as they pierce the human heart with the truth that all of humanity and creation are drawn together as one through Jesus Christ. As the time for his sacrifice drew near, the Gospel of St John tells us that Jesus prays to our Father in a way which expresses the heart of their shared plan with the Holy Spirit for each one of us:

The glory that you have given me I have given them, so that they may be one, as we are one. I in them and you in me, that they may become completely one, so that the world may know that you have sent me and have loved them even as you have loved me. (*Jn* 17:22-23)

The plan of love of the three persons of God is, therefore, to gather each of us, as scattered children, into one body with them and with one another. We are gathered to God, through knowing that we are each loved by him and called, from this knowledge, to be his love to one another. We facilitate this gathering by God of us to him and to each other once our own lives are rooted in relationships that are faithful, permanent and infused with love to the end.

This divine plan that all may be one finds its most essential expression in the covenant of marriage between a man and a woman, who by their lifelong, indissoluble, conjugal love become the most fundamental and beautiful anchor for the divine plan to gather all into one. *Gaudium et Spes*, a central document of the Second Vatican Council, expresses the importance of marriage in this way:

Through this union they experience the meaning of their oneness and attain to it with growing perfection day by day. As a mutual gift of two persons, this intimate union and the good of the children impose total fidelity on the spouses and argue for an unbreakable oneness between them.[3]

The argument for an unbreakable oneness between man

and woman, as the centrepiece of this divine plan, is both theological and anthropological. The theological foundation is expressed in what *Amoris Laetitia* describes as the "majestic early chapters of Genesis" which "present the human couple in its deepest reality".[4] Genesis states that "God created humankind in his image, in the image of God he created them; male and female he created them" (1:27). Pope Francis remarks in *Amoris Laetitia* that it is striking that the "image of God" here refers to couples – male and female.[5] In the marriage ceremony, the man and woman enter into a heightened sense of the otherness of the other sex and of marriage as a threshold into the territory of the other sex.

From an anthropological standpoint, the human person is created as man or woman and with a natural, physical and sexual complementarity through which human life is procreated and children are ideally nurtured and educated. This human ecology is intrinsic in the very cells of our bodies, which are comprised of the genetic material of our biological mother and father and of their male and female ancestors before them. Our bodies are themselves a natural, permanent, irrevocable union of man and woman. Neither man, nor woman, fully captures what it is to be human but in their union, including sexual union, man and woman capture something about the wholeness and integrity of human nature.

In 129 short talks delivered between September of 1979 and November of 1984, Pope St John Paul II gave the first major teaching project of his pontificate, which he also gave the working title of "Theology of the Body". In this teaching, he bridged the theological and the anthropological dimensions of how our oneness is realised through our creation as man and woman. He speaks of the "spousal meaning" of our bodies, which are created as a gift for each other, as we are called to unity with each other in love. To live 'spousally', as man and woman, is to offer our lives as a complete gift to one another and thereby be drawn into the unbreakable oneness of the divine plan.

In *Amoris Laetitia* Pope Francis refers to Jesus quoting from Genesis that "[t]he man shall be joined to his wife, and the two shall become one" (*Mt* 19:5; cf. *Gn* 2:24). Pope Francis states:

> The very word "to be joined" or "to cleave", in the original Hebrew, bespeaks a profound harmony, a closeness both physical and interior, to such an extent that the word is used to describe our union with God: "My soul clings to you" (*Ps* 63:8). The marital union is thus evoked not only in its sexual and corporal dimension, but also in its voluntary self-giving in love.[6]

This early observation by Pope Francis in his recent Apostolic Exhortation opens us to the redemptive reality of the marital union of man and woman. In its deepest and most truthful essence, it is a covenant with God, realised in the relationship of the couple in Jesus Christ. Man and woman are called to be truly one by becoming conformed to Christ, by being reclaimed by him, redeemed by his incomparable love through the opening of his arms upon the cross and the exposure of his heart to the utmost extent.

The oneness of marriage between a man and a woman is not a private relationship but rather one which, in its interior dimensions, is infinite, because, in being anchored in the incomparable love of Jesus Christ that is expressed in his death and resurrection, the humanity of the couple are joined to the infinity of God's love for them and for all of his creation.

The couple in marriage become redeemed, not by sacrificing their lives to each other but to their shared relationship, for the deepest identity of their relationship rests in God's eternal love. By jointly sacrificing to their shared relationship in God, the couple become rooted in an eternal covenant while becoming ever more gradually conformed to the person of Jesus Christ. As the couple become one with each other in love, they become one with God also and this "threefold cord cannot be easily broken" (*Qo* 4:12). Hans Urs von Balthasar describes this redemptive grounding of the union of man and woman in God in this way:

> As persons the spouses entrust themselves not only to the beloved "thou" and to the biological laws of fertility and family; they entrust themselves foremost to a form with which they can wholly identify themselves even in the deepest aspects of their personality because this form extends through all the levels of life – from its biological

roots up to the very heights of grace and of life in the Holy Spirit.[7]

As a man and woman grow in an interior knowledge of being loved together by God and in their love for each other, this love is called forth to join in oneness to others. Through realising their shared identity in Jesus Christ, the Holy Spirit opens their hearts to extend love to others whom they encounter. By drawing others into the hospitality of the home of their own relationship, they gather them to the home of the Father's love.

In this way, they make the body of Christ a reality through their love and incarnate the union between Christ and his Church. As they become one body in Christ, they enable the greater realisation of the oneness of the body of Christ in the larger world, which is realised in mutually supportive acts of loving kindness and of hospitality to others. Pope Francis states that the sacrament of marriage makes visible the grace granted to them "to become a domestic church and a leaven of new life for society".[8] In so doing, man and woman, as one and as one with God's incarnate love, draw all of us to each other and to God, which is the heart of the divine plan to be fulfilled in eternity.

2. The human ecology of marriage

The true meaning of marriage is rooted in the nature of the human person, or more particularly, the genesis of each one of us. Our biological origins are found in the genetic union of a man and a woman, our own mother and father. Every one of us is the indissoluble union in our bodies of the union of one man and one woman.

Humans cells contain twenty-three pairs of chromosomes, that is forty-six chromosomes per cell, with one set of twenty-three coming from one's father and the other set of twenty-three coming from one's mother. One member of each pair of chromosomes comes from the mother (through the egg cell) and the other member of each pair comes from the father (through the sperm cell). One's own body is, therefore, in every cell, other than one's red blood cells, a permanent, indissoluble union throughout one's lifetime, of the genetic, hereditary material that one receives from a man and a woman, one's own, unique father and mother. This is a biological fact. It cannot be changed. It is the very nature of who and what each one of us is.

Of the forty-six chromosomes in human cells, there are twenty-two pairs of what are called autosomes and one pair of sex chromosomes. In relation to this solitary pair of sex chromosomes, every woman has two X sex chromosomes

(XX) and every man has an X and a Y sex chromosome (XY). In females, the cells in the body have forty-six chromosomes (forty-four autosomes plus two copies of the X chromosome). In males, the cells in the body have forty-six chromosomes (forty-four autosomes plus an X and a Y chromosome). Men and woman have, therefore, twenty-two pairs of autosomes, which contain most of the hereditary information and one pair of sex chromosomes, which can be 'XX' or 'XY' and determine the sex of the person as a woman or a man.

As the sex chromosomes of a woman are XX, she can only pass on the X chromosome to her offspring. It is the father's chromosome that determines the sex of their child. If a father passes on his X chromosome, the baby will be a girl. If he passes on his Y chromosome, the baby will be a boy. The sex of the child is determined by whether the sperm that fertilises the egg is carrying another X or a Y chromosome. The sex of the human person is, therefore, determined at conception by the chromosome in the sperm of the person's father. This again is a biological, objective and scientific fact. Sexual difference between a man and a woman is based upon our genetic, inherited structure that we are given from the moment of conception.

'Intersex' is a term which describes a wide variety of combinations of what are considered male and female biology. People who are described as being 'intersex' are born with any one of several variations in sex characteristics, including chromosomes, gonads, sex hormones or genitals that do not fit with the definitions for male or female bodies. Such variations may involve genital ambiguity and combinations of the sex chromosomes other than XY-male and XX-female. Some people can be intersex by reason of unusual sex hormones which can be caused by an atypical set of sex chromosomes.

There is dispute among medical experts and scholars as to what percentage of people are intersex, because there is disagreement on what constitutes the definition of being intersex. The Intersex Society of North American states that if you ask experts at medical centres how often a child is born so noticeably atypical in terms of genitalia that a specialist in sex differentiation is called in, the number comes to about one in fifteen hundred to one in two thousand births, that is between 0.06% and 0.05% of births in North America.[9] This society also states, however, that there are a lot more people than that born with subtler forms of sex anatomy variations, some of which do not become transparent until later in life.

While there are rare exceptions of persons who are intersex – that is, having the biological features of a man and a woman – the human being is biologically created as a man or a woman. This is not some arbitrary, subjective difference that can be changed at will but a fundamental, objective, biological reality inherent in the nature of the human person. The inherent complementarity of man and woman is the most basic and intrinsic reality of human ecology, which is fully honoured in the marriage of both.

Marriage between a man and a woman recognises that the human person is divided at the most fundamental and profound level genetically as a man or a woman. In the union of man and woman, including their sexual union, they capture the fullness of human nature in a unique way and give expression to their complementary nature. The entire existence of each one of us emanates from the genetic complementarity of our mother and father. As human beings, we are procreated from the union of man and woman and as a man or a woman. By recognising that marriage is between a man and a woman, we acknowledge the truth of who we are as human beings, of how we have come into being and of how we are as human beings of one sex or the other.

Every human person is created through the union of the gametes of a man and a woman. Each one of us is formed in the womb of a woman and carry the genetic material of our own mother and father for life. Every human being longs to be nurtured by his or her own genetic, biological mother and father. We are made in this way. The protection of the unique meaning of marriage as the union of one man and one woman is inscribed in our bodies as male and female and is the cornerstone of human ecology. The first and fundamental structure for human ecology is the family, the genetic, biological, intellectual, psychological and spiritual bond between a mother, a father and their child, which marriage seeks to honour and serve. This is why Pope Francis states in *Amoris Laetitia*: "There is a failure to realise that only the exclusive and indissoluble union between a man and a woman has a plenary role to play in society as a stable commitment that bears fruit in new life" (*AL* 52).

Homosexual unions and heterosexual unions are not, therefore, equivalent social entities for the protection of the identity of the human person and the future well-being of society, because only a heterosexual union can ever, within itself:

- have the capacity for procreation and thus for the growth and development of the family unit;

- satisfy the natural right of a child to the stable society of his or her natural father, mother and siblings in family life; and

- have the potential to renew and extend the family bond through many generations and thus to build up and strengthen society.

This is also why Pope Francis states in *Amoris Laetitia* that "[w]e need to acknowledge the great variety of family situations that can offer a certain stability, but de facto or same-sex unions, for example, may not simply be equated with marriage. No union that is temporary or closed to the transmission of life can ensure the future of society" (*AL* 52).

Part Two: The denial of the objective truth of marriage

In *Amoris Laetitia*, Pope Francis makes an observation which precisely defines what has been happening in Western societies in relation to the understanding of marriage. He says:

> Many countries are witnessing a legal deconstruction of the family, tending to adopt models based almost exclusively on the autonomy of the individual will. (*AL* 53)

There are three elements in this statement, each of which enables us to gain an understanding of the context in which the truth of marriage is being destroyed by false ideas:

1. The autonomy of the individual will

2. The legal deconstruction of the family

3. The adoption of models

1. The autonomy of the individual will

For people who try to adhere to Christian belief in Western societies today, the question arises as to how we have come to a position of believing that marriage is not based on the sexual difference between a man and a woman when it is only through this difference that each of us came into this world. We need to reflect upon how we cannot see that, even though the very cells of our bodies are constituted from genetic material from our own mother and father, we refuse to recognise the natural and reasonable truth that it is preferable for a child to be raised by his or her own mother and father or, where not possible, by making a legitimate preference for the child to be raised by a man and a woman.

At the root of all of this is the denial that we are human, that we are made. The word human comes from the root words 'hum' and 'human' which come from the Latin words *humus*, meaning 'earth' and 'ground' and *humanus* which means 'man'. It is interesting to follow the change of ideas here. It begins with 'humus' – earth – and then ends with 'human' – man. In this transition we see the origin of the human person: "Dust thou art and to dust thou must return" (*Gn* 3:19).

Instead, we deny this nature of our being as creatures because of our desire to be in the apt words of Archbishop

Charles Chaput "sovereign, self-creating" selves.[10] The problem is that it is the very opposite of real Christian freedom which posits that human potential is not realised through the mirage of personal autonomy but in truthfully surrendering to the relationship with God and the service of others and the common good.

It is also a fantasy because it denies what it is to be human, that we are creatures, that we are made and that there is a Creator. The denial of being human is, therefore, inevitably associated with being secularist, that is, denying that there is any importance to be attached to a Creator in our discussion about what is truly good and best for the human person and for society. The problem with this approach is that while it is patently untrue to claim that we create ourselves, the drive for ever more autonomy and personal options is so great within us and in our culture that we will construct a whole perception of reality so as to maintain this illusion.

Through Western culture, which is no longer simply changing but is now change itself, particularly through the influence of social media, we falsely present to each other that we make ourselves and that we make our own reality. We find it next to impossible, therefore, to receive and accept revealed truth or fundamental realities about how we have been made as man or woman, which form the basis for the true meaning of marriage.

2. The legal deconstruction of the family

This radical separation of the understanding of marriage from the truth that the human person is created as man or woman finds its origins from the 1960s and 1970s onwards with the emergence of philosophical trends or movements that have become known as postmodernism and poststructuralism respectively. These philosophies underpin the false claim that the human person is a sovereign, self-creating self. They gained credence in universities in Western societies and, in turn, have influenced two generations of graduates in the study of the humanities.

Postmodernism is difficult to define because to do so violates the postmodern premise that no definite terms, boundaries or absolute truths exist. Postmodernists believe that truth is relative and that it is up to each individual to determine for himself. They posit that Christianity cannot claim primacy or dictate morals. Their approach is defined by an attitude of scepticism, irony or rejection of grand narratives and objective notions of reason, human nature and truth. Accordingly, postmodernists often assert that claims to knowledge and truth are contextual or socially constructed.

This feeds into another philosophical movement that is known as poststructuralism. This is associated with the works of a series of mid-twentieth-century French and continental philosophers and critical theorists who came to international prominence in the 1960s and 1970s. They argue that founding knowledge either on our experience (phenomenology) or systematic structures (structuralism) is impossible. For them, this purported impossibility is not meant as a failure or loss but rather as a cause for celebration and liberation. With this way of thinking, the sovereign, self-creating self can be given free rein because personal interpretation becomes all important and objective realities are rejected. There are three theorists, in particular, who can be associated with the rise of these two philosophical trends or ways of viewing reality, all of whom emanate from France. They are the psychoanalyst Jacques Lacan (1901-1981) and the philosophers Michel Foucault (1926-1984) and Jacques Derrida (1930-2004).

A major theory rejected by poststructuralists is binary opposition, such as that of man and woman. Just as postmodernism is characterised by scepticism and a denial of objective truth, poststructuralism is founded upon a critique of social or cultural constructs, such as marriage, both in terms of what it is and the language used to describe it and which, from this perspective, has to be deconstructed. Poststructuralism rejects received truth and that there is a given order in creation that simply is, which is beyond how one interprets it. These two philosophical trends have, therefore, fuelled the deconstruction of the biological ties between a man, a woman and their child in the laws of Western societies, which begins in claiming that marriage is not based on the union of a man and a woman.

3. The adoption of models

The third element of the key sentence of Pope Francis in *Amoris Laetitia* is "the adoption of models". This is an accurate name to give to the imposition of an ideology in order to assert and maintain political power. When a person or a society becomes possessed by an ideology, which Pope Francis has often neatly termed as "ideological possession", one becomes fixated upon the partial truth of one's understanding of a problem and mistakes it for the total truth. So, for example, a person argues that two people should be treated with equal respect and dignity, irrespective of their sexual orientation. The truth of this principle is then expanded into the ideology that marriage can be interpreted as applying to two people without distinction as to their sex while ignoring the larger, objective truths of the biological reality of the human person and the human ecology of marriage.

The great Catholic historian Christopher Dawson (1889-1970) wrote at the time of the rise to power of Hitler and the ideology of Nazism in Germany and during the dictatorship of Stalin and the ideology of Communism in the Soviet Union. In 1933, he wrote that civilisation is being uprooted from its foundations in nature and tradition and is being reconstituted in a new organisation which is as artificial and mechanical as a modern factory.[11] Fr Vincent Twomey, Emeritus Professor of Moral Theology at Maynooth University, Ireland, has also written that this radical cultural shift is the 'liquidation' and reconfiguration of marriage and the family, in order to facilitate a new ordering of relationships between the individual and the State – towards conformity to what he calls "a standardised type of mass civilisation".[12]

This recurring ideological struggle decouples marriage and the family from the sexual difference of man and woman. It involves an attempt to liquidate the family rooted in the central deconstruction of the nature of the human person as man or woman. We turn now to consider five particular ideological positions which seek to effect this and which have led to such a fundamental and false understanding of marriage becoming pervasive in Western societies in recent years.

Part Three: The five ideas that destroy marriage

1. Excarnation

The teaching and mission of the Catholic Church centres upon the nature of the human person being made by God in his image and likeness. This is revealed in the Book of Genesis in the Old Testament, but also in how God disclosed himself fully in the actuality, the flesh and blood of a human person, Jesus Christ, as revealed in the New Testament. This is the basis of our dignity as human beings – that we are embodied in the image and likeness of God and underwritten by the incarnation of the Son of God in human nature.

This means that each of us has a nature which is written into our human bodies. Pope Benedict XVI in his seminal address to the Bundestag at the Reichstag Building in Berlin on 22nd September 2011 spoke of this when he referred to an ecology of man. He said:

> [T]here is also an ecology of man. Man too has a nature that he must respect and that he cannot manipulate at will. Man is not merely self-creating freedom. Man does not create himself. He is intellect and will, but he is also nature,

and his will is rightly ordered if he respects his nature, listens to it and accepts himself for who he is, as one who did not create himself. In this way, and in no other, is true human freedom fulfilled.

The opposite of this is the prevailing delusion that we are not made and we are not creatures. It asserts that we make ourselves and we have no creator. Christianity completely contradicts this delusion in the most profound and beautiful way. It affirms that we are created by an almighty God but that God nonetheless became a human being, a creature. Christian faith believes that God did this to show his total empathy with our condition and through this human being, Jesus Christ, humanity is drawn back to God in the action of the Holy Spirit.

Christianity rejects the great deception of this era which is that we create ourselves rather than that we are created. For this confusion to be maintained, we must deny our existence as embodied creatures. This is what is meant by the term 'excarnation'. It is to deny that we are embodied and the objective, scientific truth of how our bodies are. There is a new alienation of the self from the flesh. Charles Taylor, the eminent Canadian philosopher, speaks about 'excarnation' of the self from bodily form and the disengagement of reason from the flesh. This false ideology needs to be countered by recognising that the human self only exists as embodied.

The human self is not a free-floating, ethereal presence as some postmodernists continuously assert. As Fr Dermot Lane has written:

> The 'I' is only available through the body and comes alive when the body is touched. Part of the problem with 'excarnation' is the persistent presence of a dualism that haunts anthropology: body and soul, spirit and matter, self and flesh.[13]

Pope St John Paul II stated that "Marriage is an institution based on natural law and its characteristics are inscribed in the very being of man and woman."[14] His teaching speaks about the spousal meaning of our bodies, which are created for love, and about a true understanding of the person – body and soul. It reveals a deeper understanding of how we live the married vocation and the celibate vocation or how to live 'spousally' by offering our lives as a gift at any age and in any situation. Gift expresses the essential truth about the human body. The physical human body can tell us about God – the fullest revelation of him being given to us in Jesus Christ, a man with a physical body. In a sense, if we have the eyes to see, our own bodies can teach us so much about God. God's impression is in each of us.

The sexual ideology that has redefined marriage and battered the family emanates from an entirely different perspective. It is based upon an inaccurate anthropology. The challenges to the truths that we are created male and female and that male and female are created for each other in marriage arise from losing sight of the true nature of the human person as embodied. Human nature finds expression in either male or female bodies. Marriage, as the intimate and permanent union of man and woman, is the unique expression and embodiment of the wholeness of human nature and should, therefore, enjoy a unique status. Neither man nor woman fully captures what it is to be human, but in their union, including sexual union, man and woman capture something about the wholeness and integrity of embodied human nature. Marriage is a celebration of the dignity of difference between man and woman and of the truth that in the encounter with somebody from the opposite sex, the embodied wholeness of human nature is revealed.

2. Gender theory

The primacy of the individual will in Western culture is perhaps most tellingly revealed in the recent emergence of 'gender theory'. It suggests that whether a person is a man or a woman is entirely a matter of personal will and not one founded on the nature of the human body.

The sexual difference between a man and a woman can be understood at three related levels which begin at birth and incrementally develop as the person matures to adulthood:

a. from birth, the fundamental, primary level of the human body – that is, the biological difference between a male or a female, referred to as a person's sex and based upon chromosomes, hormonal profiles, internal and external sex organs and bodily function;

b. the secondary level of gender, which a child increasingly becomes aware of – that is, how we give expression to being a male or a female, being the characteristics that a society or culture delineates as masculine or feminine;

c. the third level of sexual orientation, which gradually emerges in late childhood and early adolescence – that is, whether the person is attracted to a person of the opposite sex or to a person of the same sex or to both.

The sexuality of the human person can then be understood as encompassing these three different levels, with the human body, the sex of the human person, being the foundation, upon which the culture of society delineates gender, that is, what is masculine and feminine. At the more surface level of human sexuality is the sexual orientation of the human person. Though this is a profound aspect of the human person, it is not as foundational of human sexuality as one's understanding of what it is to be masculine or feminine. Again, neither of these levels are as fundamental as the embodied nature of one's sex that arises from the genetic structure of one's being.

The ideology of gender theory distorts the inter-relationship and relative importance of these different levels, which are inherent in a truthful understanding of human sexuality, by positing that one's 'gender' is chosen and need not correspond with one's biological sex. It does so by:

- denying the revealed, objective truth of the human body so that human sexuality is only understood in terms of gender and sexual orientation;

- placing excessive importance upon the sexual orientation of the human person, rendering it more foundational of human sexuality than it actually is by giving it an excessive sense of being fixed and determinative of human identity;

- engaging in a corresponding devaluing of the importance of gender and unduly rendering it as being subjective, fluid and impermanent.

In essence, gender theory denies the fundamental, objective, physical reality of the body of the human person as a man or a woman. Having removed this foundation of human identity, it then turns gender and sexual orientation upside down, making sexual orientation the foundation of human identity and one's gender something which is fluid and determined by one's own will.

The confusion of these levels also leads to a misunderstanding of being intersex with being transgender. Very few people who are transgender are intersex. Being intersex tends to centre upon having reproductive organs that are not clearly that of a male or a female. Being transgender is about a person's experience of being male or female. The vast majority of people who are transgender are born with genitals that look perfectly normal but their normal genitalia do not configure with the sex they feel they are or with their sex chromosomes (XY or XX).

This phenomenon of gender theory is described by Pope Francis in *Amoris Laetitia* when naming it as a challenge to the Christian understanding of marriage and the family. He says:

> Yet another challenge is posed by the various forms of an ideology of gender that "denies the difference and reciprocity in nature of a man and a woman and envisages a society without sexual differences, thereby eliminating the anthropological basis of the family. This ideology leads to educational programmes and legislative

enactments that promote a personal identity and emotional intimacy radically separated from the biological difference between male and female. Consequently, human identity becomes the choice of the individual, one which can also change over time".[15] It is a source of concern that some ideologies of this sort, which seek to respond to what are at times understandable aspirations, manage to assert themselves as absolute and unquestionable, even dictating how children should be raised. It needs to be emphasised that "biological sex and the socio-cultural role of sex (gender) can be distinguished but not separated".[16] (*AL* 56)

Gender theory subverts the nature of sexuality by denying the male–female complementarity encoded into our bodies. In doing so, it attacks the cornerstone of human identity and meaning and by extension, the foundation of human social organisation. Gender theory belongs within the recent and emerging philosophy of secularist posthumanism which emanates from a denial of the body, a denial of the human person as limited and created and, therefore, ultimately, a denial of God. It is driven by a belief that the human person is known by self-determination alone and must be freed from the perceived limitations of genetic make-up, family history or any eternal reference.

One can contrast this perception of human sex and gender with the teaching of Pope Francis on 15th April 2015 during his Wednesday morning catechesis in Rome when he said:

For example, I ask myself, if the so-called gender theory is not, at the same time, an expression of frustration and resignation, which seeks to cancel out sexual difference because it no longer knows how to confront it. Yes, we risk taking a step backwards. The removal of difference in fact creates a problem, not a solution. In order to resolve the problems in their relationships, men and women need to speak to one another more, listen to each other more, get to know one another better, love one another more. They must treat each other with respect and co-operate in friendship. On this human basis, sustained by the grace of God, it is possible to plan a lifelong marital and familial union. The marital and familial bond is a serious matter, and it is so for everyone, not just for believers. I would urge intellectuals not to leave this theme aside, as if it had to become secondary in order to foster a more free and just society.

3. Equalism

Western society has also become engulfed by a false ideology, an ideological possession, which arises from a misunderstanding of the principle of equality. This ideology of equality can be termed equalism. It finds specific expression in claims for same-sex marriage through the use of the slogan 'marriage equality'.

This philosophical misunderstanding of equality by its ideologues (whether in relation to marriage or otherwise) arises in three respects. Firstly, they treat equality as an absolute value which it is not. The demands of equality must be balanced with freedom of conscience and with personal responsibility. Equality, like freedom of conscience and personal responsibility, must all serve higher values such as those of truth and justice.

The second misunderstanding in equality ideology is that it omits the centrality of difference to the true meaning of equality. True equality respects genuine differences between people and resources and then seeks to reach a just balance or harmony between them. Equality ideology seeks to impose a uniformity which obliterates all difference and leaves a stifling, sterile sameness. It demands that opposite sex unions and same sex unions must be treated in the exact same way, by calling them both marriage, even though this denies the most fundamental nature of the human being as embodied as a man or a woman.

The third falsity in equality ideology is the claim that it is neutral. Behind the mask of some claims for equality in Western societies, there is invariably lurking some form of identity politics, that is, a particular grouping seeking to advance its own aims and agenda for its own good rather than that of society. Equalism is deeply secularist in that it seeks to exclude any arguments based on religion or faith that underline true differences that must be honoured which contradict its ideological assertions. It promotes a secularist ideology that says that God and faith have no role to play in the development of the human person. In this way, it can be termed as "cultural Marxism". It demands the sameness for all and dismisses religion in Marxist terms as "the opiate of the people".

Equality ideology constantly seeks to deny, rather than to honour and balance differences such as the objective, embodied differences between being a man and a woman upon which the true meaning of marriage is based. The danger of placing equality as a virtue above all others is clear from the most cursory historical consideration of this practice. The virtue of equality arrives into mainstream thinking from the end of the eighteenth century as the reverberations of the American and French revolutions were being felt. Equalism, or the promise of absolute equality, found its fullest voice with the overthrow of the Romanov dynasty in Russia in 1917 and formed the ideological basis for the emergence of Communism and the eventual domination of Stalin in Eastern Europe. Through reliance upon the principle of equality, the Chinese government justified the "one-child" policy introduced in China in 1978. Even in the last few years, when one looks at the censored televised footage of devoted public rallies for Kim Jong-Un, as they emerge from North Korea, one sees tens of thousands of people, in identical uniforms, all equal before their supreme leader. Equality, as a sole principle, divorced from other virtues, is not as attractive as might first appear.

The legal recognition of marriage as male–female does not discriminate but appropriately differentiates. Only a relationship between one man and one woman represents and embodies the fullness and integrity of human nature in its entirety. A relationship between a man and a woman and a relationship between two people of the same sex are fundamentally different. They are not the same. To name them differently and to treat their differences appropriately is a requirement of truth and justice, which are principles that include and transcend the value of equality. Truth and justice also encompass other values, such as freedom of conscience and personal responsibility, to ensure that society is just and ordered to the common good.

4. Dehumanised rights

Human rights are usually understood as rights to which human beings are entitled simply because they are human beings. They are considered to be both fundamental and natural. We do not have to do anything to merit or earn them and we are entitled to them regardless of our nationality, language, religion, location, ethnic origin, gender or sexual orientation. They are ours independent of any social status we might have or lack.

Human rights are considered universal in that they are applicable everywhere, to everyone and at every time. To be enforceable, there must be total clarity in terms of how they are defined. They must also be consistent with one another for it cannot be the case that one human right would contradict or undermine another. Examples of human rights are the right to life, to education, to practise one's religion and to freedom of expression. Marriage is also understood as a human right. Everyone is entitled to marry someone of the opposite sex. Human rights are regularly protected as legal rights in national and international law.

Internationally, there is nothing approaching universal consensus that two people of the same sex have a human right to marry. In fact, less than 12% of countries worldwide recognise same-sex marriage legally as matters stand.

While it must be accepted that this will increase, another recent trend has been the re-affirmation by Eastern European countries that marriage is between one man and one woman. On 25th March 2012, Slovenia held a referendum on a new Family Code (which equated the position of homosexual and conjugal marriages) adopted in the Slovenian parliament in June 2011. In a popular vote, 55% of voters rejected the new Family Code and 45% supported the law. The turnout was 30%.

A constitutional referendum was held in Croatia on 1st December 2013 on a proposed amendment to the Constitution to define marriage as being a union between a man and a woman, which would create a constitutional prohibition against same-sex marriage. The amendment was approved by 65.87% to 33.51% in a turnout of 37.9% of eligible voters. On 4th June 2014, the Slovak parliament approved a constitutional amendment to ban same-sex marriage, with 102 deputies for and 18 deputies against the legislation. On 7th February 2015, in Slovakia, a referendum on banning same-sex marriage was held. A low poll prevented this country's ban on same-sex marriage being further strengthened by means of a referendum proposal. It is significant, however, that over 90% of those who voted said yes to marriage as being possible only between a man and a woman.

This trend is significant because when it comes to being deprived of human rights, people and politicians in these countries have first-hand experience from their recent history as part of the Soviet Bloc. Nonetheless, they are tending towards protecting the definition of marriage as only possible between one man and one woman. These countries have retained a fundamental understanding that the sanctity of the family unit of man, woman and child is the cornerstone against the unwarranted intrusion of state power and authority and the ensuing erosion of individual freedom and conscience.

Similarly, the most recent decision by the European Court of Human Rights on the issue of whether same-sex 'marriage' is a human right is the case of Hämäläinen v. Finland in which judgment was given by the European Court of Human Rights on 16th July 2014. The Court reaffirmed that the European Convention on Human Rights cannot be interpreted "as imposing an obligation on Contracting States to grant same-sex couples access to marriage". Accordingly, in European Human Rights law, there is no basis for the contention that 'same-sex' marriage is a human right. At the same time, in this judgment, the Court has clearly asserted the fundamental right of a man and a woman to marry.

When we proceed to claim human rights without reference to the human person being embodied, we create dehumanised rights. When the nature and integrity of the human body is forgotten about as the universal cornerstone for determining what a human right is, it is invariably the case that dehumanised or disembodied rights claims favour adult autonomy at the expense of a different group in society who do not have the same political power – children.

By redefining marriage, without distinction as to sex, the rights of children to nurture and care from a man and a woman are side-lined. For instance, the humanity of the child to know his or her own mother and father is conflicted by conferring the status of marriage and the ensuing rights of reproduction through reproductive technologies (through the purchase of gametes – sperm and eggs – and surrogacy) upon two people of the same sex who are treated in law as a married couple. This is not, however, in accordance with the natural understanding of how a child is conceived by the union of a man and a woman and then nurtured by a mother and a father. It is the utmost vindication of a 'right' of an adult to have a child (which has no natural or legal authority whatsoever) with a corresponding denial of the right of a child to a mother and a father and to the relationships with his or her natural siblings, grandparents and wider family.

This right of a child is fundamental to the dignity of the human person. It protects the humanity of the child and prepares him or her for adulthood. This natural right is also asserted clearly in international law as it is explicitly provided for in the United Nations Convention on the Rights of the Child which entered into force on 2nd September 1990. Article 7.1 of the Convention provides that the child shall be registered immediately after birth and shall have the right from birth to a name, the right to acquire a nationality and, "as far as possible, the right to know and be cared for by his or her parents."

A similar misapplication of human rights as not referenced to the distinction as to sex between a man and a woman is faced by adoption agencies. Nobody has a right to adopt a child though agencies have a duty to find suitable parents for the children in their care. It is argued, however, that same sex couples have the same right to adopt children as any opposite sex couple and that no adoption agency can discriminate against same sex couples who apply to be adoptive parents. Sir Roger Scruton the English philosopher has noted that a complex moral question concerning the welfare of children and the duties of their guardians is surrendered to the human rights idea and all competing duties are disregarded. He says that a disembodied claim of human rights, divorced from natural law, "privileges the living over the unborn and sees submission to the will of God as valid only if it amounts to doing your own thing." He also rightly highlights that it will require courage and a measure of defiance to challenge the growing list of phoney human rights.[17]

A Christian cannot remain silent about the legal deconstruction of marriage and the right of a child, as far as is possible, to know and be cared for by his or her own mother and father. Such silence, or even advocacy for the legal deconstruction of this most fundamental unit in human nature, can be contrasted with the courage of others who do understand the nature of the challenge to give leadership on increasing consciousness in the development of human rights. One such person is Dr Habib Malik, Associate Professor of History and

Cultural Studies, Lebanese American University, Lebanon. After the Second World War, his father, Charles Malik, was centrally involved with Eleanor Roosevelt, René Cassin of France and a group of others in drafting the thirty articles of the Universal Declaration of Human Rights and its preamble. Dr Malik has made the following observation concerning how the Universal Declaration of Human Rights came into being:

> Something like the concept of natural law became extremely important in framing the Universal Declaration as opposed to positive law which is man-made and changeable but natural law is always there and pretty much eternal and tuning into that bedrock feature of the human condition, I think, became the driving, as it were, impetus for the Universal Declaration and my late father was very much of that tradition.
>
> Unfortunately, with time, human rights proliferated into a kind of a cottage industry where almost every minority, whether integral or pseudo, began to demand rights, as it were, and some of those were not necessarily human rights in the conventional sense but in a sense privileges for groups who were simply overreaching the sanctity of the union of marriage with the idea of creating a family and procreating. These are features that go beyond the State, beyond positive law, beyond legislation and the problem we face today is this confusion between where the limits of positive law should be and where the sanctity of natural law must remain and reside and be upheld.[18]

This observation of Dr Malik awakens us to how the source of human rights in the dignity of the human body has been lost and how the entire concept of human rights has been captured by certain groups to advance their own particular concerns. His statement helps us to understand how this capture has been effected in that natural rights, founded in natural law, which are universal, indivisible and timeless, have been limited to an interpretation of human rights which is not in service of human dignity and has therefore led to their becoming dehumanised. If human rights advocacy groups are to be freed from the capture of being a variety of cottage industries, they need to be anchored on a secure foundation. They need in fact to return to their ultimate origin, which is human dignity, which itself is founded in the truth that the human person is made in the image and likeness of God. The protection of the natural and sacred bond between man, woman and child must be at the heart of any true human rights project because it is the cradle of human dignity.

5. Adolescent progressivism

Most Western societies are now defined by what can be termed as a 'secularist frame'. The word 'secular' derives from the Latin word *saecularis* meaning worldly, temporal, of a generation, belonging to an age. A secularist society is one which believes it can define itself by its own era alone. Received wisdom, from previous generations, counts for little as do theories about the consequences of that society's actions for future generations. A frame is created which brackets out the past and the future. Accordingly, when this secularist frame is applied to our understanding of marriage, for instance, it matters for nothing that every other previous generation and civilisation, with a recorded history, treated marriage as a sex-based partnership between men and woman. Similarly, as the consequences of allowing for one-sex marriage are not immediately obvious and apparent at this time, the question of future adverse consequences is also blocked out from our evaluation as to the prudence or otherwise of redefining marriage.

The secularist frame further blocks out any reference to a timeless reality, to God, to a transcendent truth, to universal, eternal values. Just as there is no reference to the past or the future, there is equally no reference to an overarching narrative or to a transcendent anchor, either of which may discommode our framing of the top and bottom of our perspective. The simple and universal truths that the human person is made, that he or she is made male or female and can only be made by a male and female, are then framed outside of the debate. Once these basic, timeless truths are excluded, the way is clear inside this limited frame to simply define marriage as a permanent relationship between two people and nothing more and to then engage in a mechanistic application of the principle of equality.

The secularist frame works, therefore, to condition our perception of reality by blocking out or distorting the dimensions of:

- the past (tradition, history and experience);
- the future (the consequences of our actions for the welfare of generations to come);
- the grounding of creation and our grounding, as the created, in nature and in biological realities;
- the limitless ceiling opening to an overarching narrative, a timeless order and universal values.

In so doing, this conditioned way of seeing reality promotes the central untruth that we are not made and that we make ourselves, being the necessary delusion so as to allow for personal autonomy and the maximum optionality. The difficulty with a society that seeks to promote endless personal options, however, is that it will resist any thinking to opt out from it, to question its limits, to see that it is based on a faulty understanding of the human person. This limited way of understanding humanity, culture and society has been termed by the Canadian philosopher Charles Taylor as "exclusive humanism".

Once this falsehood takes hold, the human ego is supreme. The wisdom for the past and concern for the future are forgotten. The humility of understanding one's earthedness in nature and one's complete dependence upon God are no longer appreciated. By subscribing to the belief that there is no universal truth, no transcendent anchor, no overarching narrative, it is simply not true that one is then liberated from oppressive religious beliefs. Instead, one is imprisoned by the new walls of the secularist frame. The name of the prison is pure relativism.

This pervasive philosophy demands that we see one viewpoint as being as good as another and that we must respect all views equally. To differentiate in any way is to wrongfully discriminate. Equality is not just the supreme value but also the exclusive one in the prison of relativism. It stipulates that a relationship between two men or two women should be seen as equal to a relationship of a man and woman. Even though only the latter can involve an integration of both sexes, bring forth new life and provide natural bonds between the child and his parents as the primary educators of his life, the confines of these prison walls demand that we must treat all partnerships of two people as one and the same.

Within the secularist frame, once a minority group successfully advocates that it is not being treated the same as another group – that is, identity politics – the common good can then be placed at risk so as to meet the demand of this minority. This is achieved in the debate about the nature of marriage by blocking out the totality of what is at issue. Firstly, the secularist frame is used to define marriage as simply a permanent partnership between two people and no more than this. When you have convinced the majority of this, any attempt to exclude two people from marriage is self-evidently discriminatory. What has happened here, of course, is that all of the elements that differentiate a partnership between two people of the one sex and two of the opposite sex have been framed out of the discussion. Once you take away the embodied sex of the human person, sexual complementarity and the ability to procreate, parent and educate one's own natural children, the basis for an entirely fair, reasonable and necessary differentiation is lost and the secularist frame for the untruthful claim of discrimination is made.

The collapse of the distinction between differentiation and discrimination is caused by indifferentism. This is the untruthful denial of genuine differences between two realities so as to ensure that they are given the same recognition and status. Treating a one-sex relationship and a relationship of both sexes as being the same for the purpose of defining marriage is pure indifferentism. It has serious consequences which we cannot truly foresee. It means that when a child is being considered for adoption, one has to be indifferent as to whether the child has a mother and a father or simply two mothers or two fathers. An infant in school must be taught that marriage between a man and a woman or between two men or two women are all one and the same. Ultimately, the difference between the male and the female, the most fundamental difference of the human person, becomes a matter of indifference.

As indifferentism becomes all pervasive, another inevitable consequence is that those who highlight that truthful differences are not being honoured are shouted down, bullied into silence and labelled as ignorant and intolerant. This results in a universal distortion of conscience by what Pope Francis has described as the dictatorship of only one permitted way of thinking. The Italian language that he used says it more concisely: "la dittatura del pensiero unico". "Today you must think this way and if you don't think this way you are not modern, you are not open."[19]

Pope Francis described this dictatorship as "the modern spirit of adolescent progressivism". Like true adolescents, we reject all authority but we cannot surrender to a deeper, truer understanding of who we are, where we come from, how we are sustained and what happens when we die – the meaning and destiny of our lives. In this adolescent culture, we create our own truth. We make the truth conform to what we want.

Marriage can thus be made to what we say it is, to what suits us. It has no universal, unchanging nature that we receive, such as that it is between a male and a female. In the spirit of adolescent progressivism, we can make of it what we will. Everything can be changed because there is no anchor to a universal, unchanging truth. Marriage is something which should conform to us and not something which we should conform to.

The battle over what is the true meaning of marriage is between two irreconcilable views of reality. The first view is true and adult – that is, that everything has an inherent nature, an inbuilt purpose, that is ordered to ends that inhere in their essence and make them what they are. The second view is wrong and adolescent – that is, that things do not have a nature with ends, they are nothing in themselves and we can make of them what we wish according to our own wills and desires. This is adolescent progressivism and falsely suggests that we can make everything, including ourselves, into anything. The first view leads to the primacy of reason in human affairs and does not allow for marriage between two people of the one sex. The second view leads to the primacy of the will and allows for anything.

Conclusion:
The age of sin against the Creator

During the first day of his visit to Poland on Wednesday 27th July 2016, Pope Francis met with the bishops of Poland in the Cathedral of Kraków. On the following Tuesday, 2nd August 2016, the Vatican released what he said, which included the following:

> We are experiencing a moment of the annihilation of man as the image of God. I would like to conclude with this aspect, since behind all this there are ideologies. In Europe, America, Latin America, Africa, and in some countries of Asia, there are genuine forms of ideological colonisation taking place. And one of these – I will call it clearly by its name – is [the ideology of] 'gender'. Today children – children! – are taught in school that everyone can choose his or her sex. Why are they teaching this? Because the books are provided by the persons and institutions that give you money. These forms of ideological colonisation are also supported by influential countries. And this is terrible!
>
> In a conversation with Pope Benedict, who is in good health and very perceptive, he said to me: "Holiness, this is the age of sin against God the Creator." He is very perceptive. God created man and woman; God created the world in a certain way...and we are doing the exact opposite. God gave us things in a 'raw' state, so that we

could shape a culture; and then with this culture, we are shaping things that bring us back to the 'raw' state! Pope Benedict's observation should make us think. "This is the age of sin against God the Creator". That will help us.

The separation of marriage from the distinction as to sex between a man and a woman is the cornerstone of a radically new legal edifice, which is unhinged from the natural ecology of human sexuality and procreation. This is achieved in different countries by legally redefining our understanding of man and woman, who the parents of a child are and what a human family is. Taken together, the civil laws of different countries can now provide that:

- an adult is not necessarily a man or a woman but can choose, without any medical evidence, to go from one to the other and obtain a gender recognition certificate to this effect;

- as marriage can now be civilly contracted without distinction as to sex, one spouse, or indeed both spouses, can change their sex and this has no effect on the legal validity of their marriage – in other words if you are married and your spouse changes his or her sex, you have no entitlement to have the marriage annulled or to seek a divorce by reason of this;

- the complementarity of a mother and a father is no longer understood in the civil laws of different jurisdictions as having a value that would, all other factors being equal, allow a preference for two persons of the opposite sex over two persons of the same sex when it comes to determining what is in the best interests of a child.

The cumulative effect of such laws is to uproot our legal understanding of the family from its basis in the biological sex of the human person as a man or a woman and the sexual complementarity of both of them. It detaches our understanding of procreation as requiring a man and a woman. It denies that a child needs the care of a mother and a father. This is the legal deconstruction of the natural and Christian understanding of the family. It is a rebellion against how we are created.

This rebellion is founded upon the denial of the primary importance of the biological differences between men and women. It leads to the legal deconstruction of the family as founded upon the natural society of man and woman and the children born through their union. As human life comes from the union of male and female and is formed by it, every person yearns for a loving relationship with his or her own natural mother and father, or where not possible, to be parented and nurtured by another man and woman. It is upon this fundamental benchmark for human identity that the natural meaning of marriage is based. To contradict the natural meaning of marriage with a different legal meaning, however well-intentioned, inevitably brings about a disintegration of human identity, parenting, education and society. Pope Francis aptly affirms this in *Amoris Laetitia* in this way:

No one can think that the weakening of the family as that natural society founded on marriage will prove beneficial to society as a whole. The contrary is true: it poses a threat to the mature growth of individuals, the cultivation of community values and moral progress of cities and countries. There is a failure to realise that only the exclusive and indissoluble union between a man and a woman has a plenary role to play in society as a stable commitment that bears fruit in new life. (*AL* 52)

The understanding of marriage in Christianity seeks, therefore, to define and honour marriage as:

a. a life-long union between a man and woman, in which the couple are called to appreciate and care for all of the varied dimensions of their relationship, whether affective, sexual, intellectual or otherwise and;

b. the natural and optimum environment for the procreation, nurturing and education of children because every human person has a fundamental right and need for a mother and a father and comes from both.

The Christian tradition also offers a third understanding of marriage, which builds upon the nature of the sexual difference of man and woman and the fact that it is only through this difference that another human person can be born:

c. the integrity of man, woman and child, held within a loving relationship between all of them, is the greatest work of God because it is the clearest and most beautiful expression, in human terms, of the Holy Trinity, the integrity of three divine persons in love. As every single human being is always first a child, this incomparable expression of God in human terms is lived out in every single person's life from conception onwards.

In *Amoris Laetitia*, Pope Francis also notes that it is one thing to be understanding of human weakness and the complexities of life and another to accept ideologies that attempt to sunder what are inseparable aspects of reality. He gives profound counsel when he says:

> Let us not fall into the sin of trying to replace the Creator. We are creatures, and not omnipotent. Creation is prior to us and must be received as a gift. At the same time, we are called to protect our humanity, and this means, in the first place, accepting it and respecting it as it was created. (*AL* 56)

Above all, this Apostolic Exhortation of Pope Francis calls us to be joyful about the Gospel of the Family, for the Christian truth about marriage and parenthood is written into the fabric of every human being. Each of us comes from a mother and a father, a man and a woman. Our mothers and fathers and all of their preceding generations are knitted into our very being. This is the way we have been made by God.

> Know that the Lord is God;
> it is he that has made us and we are his. (*Ps* 99 [100]:3)

Endnotes

[1] 1983 *Code of Canon Law* of the Catholic Church, originally published on 25th January 1983, Book IV Function of the Church, Part 1 The Sacraments, Title VII. Marriage (Cann. 1055-1165).

[2] Pastoral Constitution of the Church in the Modern World *Gaudium et Spes*, 7th December 1965, promulgated by his Holiness, Pope Paul VI, note 48.

[3] Ibid.

[4] Post-Synodal Apostolic Exhortation *Amoris Laetitia* of the Holy Father Francis, On Love in the Family, April 2016, Chapter 1, paragraph 10.

[5] Ibid.

[6] Ibid at Chapter 1, paragraph 13.

[7] Hans Urs von Balthasar, *The Glory of the Lord: A Theological Aesthetics, Vol. III: Studies in Theological Style: Lay Styles* (Ignatius Press, 1982).

[8] *Amoris Laetitia*, above n 4, Chapter 8, paragraph 292.

[9] Taken from the website of the Intersex Society of North America, *www.isna.org*

[10] Charles J Chaput, OFM, Cap, Archbishop of Philadelphia, 2016 Tocqueville Lecture, University of Notre Dame, 15th September 2016.

[11] Christopher Dawson, "Christianity and Sex" in *Enquiries into Religion and Culture* (The Catholic University of America Press, 1933) 259.

[12] D Vincent Twomey, *Moral Theology after* Humanae Vitae*: Fundamental Issues in Moral Theory and Sexual Ethics* (Four Courts Press, Dublin, 2010).

[13] Dermot A Lane, *Catholic Education in the Light of Vatican II and Laudato Si'* (Veritas, Dublin, 2015) 67.

[14] Pope St John Paul II, Address to Roman Rota, 1991.

[15] *Relatio Finalis: Synod 15 – Mission of the Family in the Chirch and in the Contemporary World*. 2015, 8.

[16] Ibid, 58.

[17] Sir Roger Scruton, "The Religion of Rights" BBC Radio 4, 1st September 2017, *https://www.roger-scruton.com/articles/469-the-religion-of-rights-bbc-radio-4-1-sept-17*

[18] Taken from *The Humanum Series* Part 6: Marriage, Culture and Civil Society, *http://www.eccefilms.com/humanum*

[19] Pope Francis, Morning Meditation, 10th April 2014.

Without our loyal supporters we would not be here today.

Help us to fight spiritual hunger

Could provide four young people with booklets on prayer and vocation

Could help CTS invest in new catechesis materials for families

Could help us further develop our work with prison chaplaincies

CTS relies on the generosity of its supporters to carry out its mission.

SUPPORT US TODAY:

Call: +44 (0)20 7640 0042
Email: fundraising@ctsbooks.org
Go to: www.ctsbooks.org/give

Gods truth beautifully told.
SINCE 1868.